DATE DUE

Trendsetter

Have You Got What It Takes to Be a Fashion Designer?

by Lisa Thompson

Compass Point Books ✦ Minneapolis, Minnesota

First American edition published in 2008 by
Compass Point Books
3109 West 50th Street, #115
Minneapolis, MN 55410

Editor: Julie Gassman
Designer: Bobbie Nuytten
Creative Director: Keith Griffin
Editorial Director: Nick Healy
Managing Editor: Catherine Neitge
Content Adviser: Amy Michelle Freeman, Clothing Designer/Owner,
            SoHo Exchange, Inc., Minneapolis, Minnesota

Editor's note: To best explain careers to readers, the author has
created composite characters based on extensive interviews and research.

This book was manufactured with paper containing
at least 10 percent post-consumer waste.
Printed in the United States of America.

Library of Congress Cataloging-in-Publication Data
Thompson, Lisa, 1969-
  Trendsetter: have you got what it takes to be a fashion designer? / by Lisa Thompson.
     p. cm.
  Includes index.
  ISBN 978-0-7565-3622-0 (library binding)
  1. Fashion design—Vocational guidance—Juvenile literature. 2. Fashion designers—
Juvenile literature. I. Title.
  TT507.T468 2008
  746.9'2023—dc22   2007035559

Image Credits: Shutterstock/Alexander Gitlits, cover (left); Corbis/Gareth Brown,
cover (right). All other images are from one of the following royalty-free sources:
Big Stock Photo, Dreamstime, Istock, Photo Objects, Photos.com, and Shutterstock.
Every effort has been made to contact copyright holders of any material reproduced in
this book. Any omission will be rectified in subsequent printings if notice is given to
the publishers.

Visit Compass Point Books on the Internet at *www.compasspointbooks.com*
or e-mail your request to *custserv@compasspointbooks.com*

Table of Contents

The Chance I've Been Waiting For

I'm Chloe Long, fashion designer. I own my own label, Hype, and I've just gotten the most incredible news. I received an e-mail confirming my place at Fashion Week. It is a dream come true.

So much to do! My mind is spinning with ideas. Maybe I'll do 1970s hippie-inspired clothes, or ... how about a military theme? No, I think I'll go for rock star style! That's perfect for Hype. We're a street label for guys and girls.

To: Chloe Long, fashion designer@Hype
Subject: Fashion Week
Sent: June 6th

Dear Chloe,
We are pleased to offer you a show at next
Fashion Week.

Your show will be on February 5
timeslot. You will be required
a but without knowing wha

You must bring at least four type
that include ridiculous clothes and a
east entra

Property of
Chloe Leong,
creator and
fashion designer
of
hype

the coolest street label around!

I have to get started on designs. I want the tops to have attitude and the pants to be comfortable, yet stylish. The clothes should feel loose and casual, but look cool.

I think I'll use lots of racer red and jet black for that rocker look. I want to use funky stenciling and prints. I have some ideas based on some posters I saw during my last trip to New York.

Perhaps an Army theme?

Rock star style? Yes, that's it!

I have to start sketching right now!

Then there is the fashion show to organize. I will need a theme for the show, and I'll need someone to produce it. I'll also need a stylist, and hair and makeup artists. And what about the music?

I need to write a big list of things to do and call my team together. It's time for action!

I want my fashion show to be professional yet exciting.

5

Action Time

Designing clothes is only one part of running a fashion label. You also need to know how to make the clothes and sell them. It helps if you have good skills in pattern making and sewing. That way you can make your ideas become a reality yourself!

That's often how fashion designers start—doing everything themselves. The designing, pattern making, sewing, and selling are all done by one person. It works if you are doing a few pieces and small collections. I used to do it all myself, too, but now my business is too big for one person to manage. Most designers then build a team, like the one I have here at Hype. The team helps me run the fashion label.

Which colors will work best?

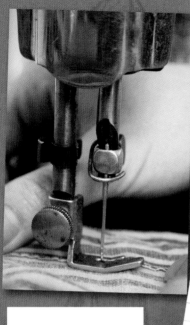

To do:

√ research current fashion trends
√ collect images of rock star style
√ come up with lots of ideas
√ decide which ideas work best
√ choose color schemes
√ start sketching designs
√ organize my team
√ hire people to work on our show

>hype

Meet the Team

Designer/creative director

As the creative director, I come up with the ideas and designs for the label. I sketch the designs, decide on the number and type of garments (items of clothing), and choose the fabric and trims.

I'm in charge of the look of Hype and create the style of our clothes. It is my job to be aware of trends and to give the label an original direction.

S M L

We need all sizes for our collection.

Pattern makers

Eva makes the patterns from my design sketches. She makes several sizes of each pattern (this is called grading) so the design is ready to be made.

Eva—the pattern genius

Sample maker

Julianna is a whiz on the sewing machine. She sews together the prototype (sample) of a new design with fabric cut from the pattern that Eva has created. Julianna also gives us production information, such as how long a garment will take to make, the best way to make it, and the costs involved.

PUN FUN

When the designer was asked how a suit was coming, she replied, "Sew far, sew good."

Sample models

Skye and Noah are our contract models. They come in when we need them to try on sample clothes. Then we can see what works and what needs to be changed. This is very important. Sometimes you can have an idea that looks good on paper, but when you put it on a real person, it looks awful.

Noah is our male model.

Skye loves modeling my new designs.

Production manager

Once we are happy with the garments, Jason plans the mass production of them. There are lots of things to organize to ensure things run as smoothly as possible.

Fabric is ordered from wholesalers and textile mills. Sometimes fabric needs to be printed, dyed, or embroidered before it is cut. This is also Jason's job to organize.

Jason makes sure all the deliveries come in on time and the quality standards of our clothes are met. It's a big job—he has to be very organized!

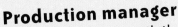

Jason coordinates all parts of the production process.

A textile loom

I think I want attitude for my collection!

Business manager

Robert manages Hype's finances. He makes sure we have money to run the company and pay our staff and suppliers.

Robert also helps me look after our buyers. He is always looking for new clients and places to promote and sell Hype. Robert places advertisments for Hype to get our buyers and the press interested and excited about what we're creating.

Where's it made?

Most clothing is made outside a company's headquarters and often outside the country.

The patterns and the fabric are sent to the cutters, who cut out the fabric pieces. These pieces then go to the seamstresses, along with all the various trims, such as zippers, buttons, thread—everything they will need to make the clothing.

How I Became a Fashion Designer

I think the sunglasses make the outfit!

I've always loved clothes and dressing up. Even when I was younger, I was forever putting outfits together. I made sure I had the right shoes, jewelry, and bag to go with every outfit.

The first person who taught me about fashion design was my mom. She would make new outfits for me and my sister nearly every weekend. Some were very, very strange!

My sister looked wild that summer.

Mom gave me some fashion tips.

How does it look?

In high school, I studied textile design. In my spare time, I would sketch and make outfits for my friends. After graduating, I wanted to learn more about fashion, so I enrolled in a fashion technology course in college.

During my final year in college, I began selling my designs at a local flea market. When I got my degree, I kept selling my clothes there and even persuaded some stores in the area to carry my designs, too.

One day, a buyer for a chain of streetwear stores saw my clothes at the flea market. He asked whether I would be able to make clothes for his stores and gave me his card.

Selling in a flea market is a great way to start.

The Street clothing
John Thomas
Buyer
530 West 24th Street, Suite 14
New York, New York 10001
212/555-1234

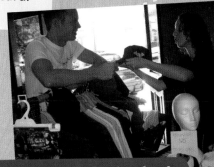

Getting my clothes into local stores was a real breakthrough.

When I called him the next day and he told me how many items he wanted, I nearly fell over. It was five times as much as I was used to producing. I quickly realized that to fill the order I would need financial help.

I needed money to get started in the big time.

SIGN HERE

name (print)

signature

A family friend decided to invest in my business with me, and Hype was born. It is often stressful and always a lot of work. But seeing someone walking down the street in one of my designs is a huge buzz. It makes all the effort worthwhile.

A Background for Fashion

Most people become designers by studying design in college. They learn about technical and artistic aspects of fashion design.

After college, many designers begin their careers working as design assistants in fashion houses. Fashion assistants normally work in the fashion room alongside the pattern cutters, sample seamstresses, and other designers.

Some designers have had no formal fashion training. They just started making and selling clothes.

However, the fashion business is very competitive. Fashion design is a production-focused job that involves meetings, deadlines, budgeting, negotiating with suppliers, stress, and long hours. To succeed, designers need a good business sense, as well as a natural flair for fashion design.

It takes a lot of determination and skill to get your clothes hanging in the stores.

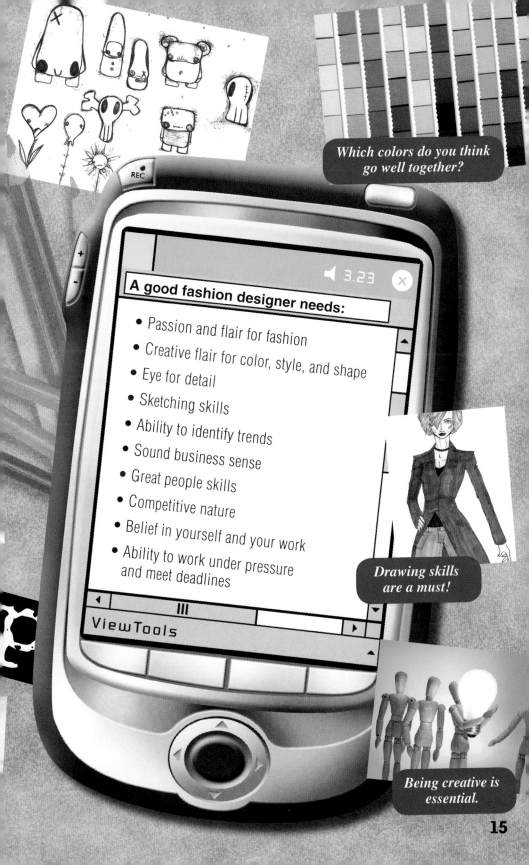

Which colors do you think go well together?

A good fashion designer needs:

◀ 3.23 ✕

- Passion and flair for fashion
- Creative flair for color, style, and shape
- Eye for detail
- Sketching skills
- Ability to identify trends
- Sound business sense
- Great people skills
- Competitive nature
- Belief in yourself and your work
- Ability to work under pressure and meet deadlines

View Tools

Drawing skills are a must!

Being creative is essential.

Fashion—Step by Step

There are many steps in producing a garment. This is what happens from the first idea to the finished product.

STEP 1 — Think of styles, get inspired

STEP 2 — Research styles and ideas

STEP 3 — Sketch designs

STEP 4 — Choose fabrics and trim

STEP 5 — Finalize designs

STEP 6 — Make patterns

STEP 7 — Sampling and fitting cycle

STEP 8 — Create sample collection and style book

STEP 9 — Show collection to buyers

STEP 10 — Buyers place orders

STEP 11

Full-scale production begins

- Check and grade patterns
- Receive and check fabrics
- Spread fabrics and cut garments
- Bundle cut garments into sizes and styles
- Send cut work to seamstresses
- Finish garments—buttons and buttonholes
- Cleaning and pressing
- Quality control
- Tagging and packing

STEP 12

Send to retailers

STEP 13

Check and price garments

special value
$59⁹⁰
select styles

STEP 14

Create retail displays

STEP 15

The consumer buys garments

The Creative Process

Designers have various ways of working. Some sketch their ideas on paper. Others work directly with the fabric itself, draping and folding it until they find the right shape. Or they adapt patterns from previous collections.

I consider the following when designing a garment:

- Who will wear the garment?
- When will it be worn (which season)?
- What is the cost of producing the garment?

Take a peek inside.

My journals— lots of ideas in there!

Initial inspiration

I carry a journal everywhere I go. That way, if I get a flash of inspiration, I can just jot it down. My journals are full of ideas, scribbles, pictures, photos, invitations, and clippings—anything that catches my eye.

I keep most of my research in my journals, too. I look out for new colors, fabrics, trims, and accessories. This is called trend forecasting.

High-tech style gurus

Like many designers, I get a lot of my information and inspiration from Internet trend services. These companies, like the Worth Global Style Network (*www.wgsn.com*), provide up-to-the-minute information on the latest popular styles from around the world. News, research, and photographs show everything from catwalk shows in Milan and celebrities in Rio to what people are wearing on the streets of Amsterdam.

It's a way for modern style industries, including fashion, cosmetics, and interior design, to keep a finger on the pulse of what's new, hip, and happening. And all this can be done without having to travel to many countries each year, which takes time and money.

> *Your computer is your best friend. Know how to use it.*

The drawing board

Sometimes I draw my designs by hand. At other times I use my computer, using design programs like Photoshop or Illustrator. With these programs, I can easily change the color or fabric of a design to see what it would look like.

Send / Receive

PUN FUN — **The third-generation clothes designer had it in her jeans.**

19

Types of Fashion

Nearly all fashion items fit into one of three types: the fad, the standard, and the classic.

The fad
This is the latest craze. The fad garment generally lasts one or two seasons. Examples are fluffy leg warmers and gaucho pants.

The standard
These items are the look of the season. These dresses, shirts, and pants will reflect the current season's style, cut, color, and fabric.

The classic
This constant, functional, and versatile item never goes out of style. Examples are the little black dress, the blazer, and the trench coat.

Why we wear what we do

Certain clothes and fashion styles are worn for particular reasons:

- **A special occasion**: Such as a wedding dress to get married
- **Cultural tradition**: Such as a kimono in Japan or kilts in Scotland
- **Religious reasons**: Such as wearing a Jewish yarmulke (skull cap)
- **Practicality**: Such as the parkas Inuits wear in their frozen homeland
- **To make a fashion statement**: Such as punk or gothic styles

The House of Worth

Charles Frederick Worth (1826–1895) is regarded as the first fashion designer. Before he set up his fashion house in Paris, clothing design and creation were done by seamstresses. High fashion was influenced by styles worn in the royal courts.

Worth broke with the tradition of customers' dictating the design. He asked customers to choose from his own designs, which he displayed on models at shows.

Because of his success, customers would attach a label with his name to his designs. The customers wanted others to know that the clothes were from the House of Worth. This started the tradition of designers' being not only the creative heads of fashion houses, but the symbols of brands as well.

1883 Paris fashion

21

Fashion Themes

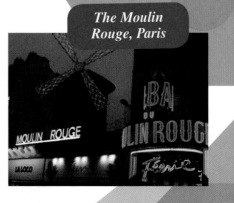

The Moulin Rouge, Paris

Each fashion collection has an overall theme. Designing around themes gives me a focus. Themes might be inspired by a place in the world, a specific subculture, or even a movie. Examples include the Moulin Rouge or cowboys in the West ... or rock stars!

Themes allow the garments to have a similar feel and look. That way, all the fabrics and colors that make up the collection look as if they belong together.

There are categories of clothes within each themed collection. Categories group garments around their functions (sportswear, casual, etc.). For these categories, I don't just design the clothes. I design the total look, including bags, hats, or jewelry. In fact, I create any accessories I think should go with the clothes.

Accessories for a chic style

Accessories for a bohemian look

22

The categories for my rock star themed collection are:

On the street: Clothes for chilling out, such as cargo pants and T-shirts; they're casual but cool

Free style: Sporty/functional clothes, such as hoodies and track pants; these pieces combine comfort with looking good

After dark: Clothes for going out, such as funky shirts and tops, and bold trousers, skirts and dresses; really out there

I did some research and sketching on rock star style during my last vacation in New York. I try to go on inspirational trips to fashion capitals around the world—London, New York, Tokyo, Paris, or Milan. Every city has a different take on fashion. Paris and Milan are about classic style and elegance. In contrast, New York, London, and Tokyo are more about taking fashion risks and creating bold new designs. Seeing what's happening out there helps get my creative juices flowing!

Tokyo has a confident and crazy take on fashion.

Beautiful Milan

Greetings from London

Welcome to New York

23

Color, Texture, and Pattern

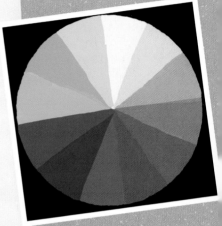

Color

Color is a Hype trademark. I use bright color combinations, such as:

- pink/orange
- blue/green
- purple/ lime

I keep a color-wheel picture on my desk for reference.

For unique colors, our fabrics are dyed beforehand. I figure out the fabrics, colors, and trims that we will use. Then I create storyboards so everyone knows what goes with what.

Trim includes anything other than fabric that we add onto garments, such as zippers, buttons, ties, and beads.

Tie-dying in action

My storyboards have all the information we need to create the clothes.

Color, color, and more color

In fashion lingo, colors fall into four main groups: staple, seasonal, fashion, and accent

- **Staple colors**: Colors that are used every year and are liked by all age groups in all seasons. These include black, white, navy blue, and gray.

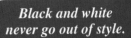

Black and white never go out of style.

- **Seasonal colors**: Colors that remind us of certain times of the year:
  light + bright colors = summer
  warm + dark colors = winter

Warm browns keep us snug in winter.

- **Fashion colors**: Colors that dominate each fashion season and vary from year to year. One year pastels might be in. The next it could be neutral, nature-inspired colors.

- **Accent colors**: Small amounts of color that contrast with the main one, like a green zipper on a red jacket.

Accent colors give clothes an interesting look.

You can come up with thousands of color schemes using new shades made by mixing standard colors.

Color crazy

- **Monochrome** colors are shades of the same color, like dark blue, mid-blue, and light blue.

A monochrome shirt has multiple shades of blue.

- **Complementary** colors bounce off each other. They sit on opposite sides of the color wheel, like blue and orange.

Orange and blue are complementary colors.

- **Harmonious** colors are on either side of a main color on the color wheel, like yellow-orange and yellow-green on either side of yellow.

25

Texture

Texture means the feel of something; for example, smooth, grainy, or silky. Texture is important for clothes because we touch them, wear them, and look at them, so I need to get it just right. Fabric plays a large part in creating texture.

A good knowledge of fabrics is essential for designing and making clothes. I must consider how clothes feel, how they sit on the body, how long they last, and how they should be cared for.

Fabrics come in many types, and fabric producers are always coming up with new materials. For example, they can be knitted, woven, or felted.

Texture can be created with trims, such as patches, beads, or buttons. Ribbon threaded through garments, ruffles, pleating, and quilting also affect the feel and look of clothes.

Pattern

Pattern is another factor in fashion design. Patterns can be very seasonal—one year animal prints are in, the next it can be spots or stripes. I love making up different patterns for fabric.

You can use swirls, polka dots, retro-style paisley print, or floral designs, to name just a few. For the new Hype collections, I'm thinking of using stripes and plaids. We'll see!

Fabric and fibers

Fabric threads are called fibers. Fibers can be either natural or manufactured. Examples of natural fibers are cotton, linen, wool, and silk. Examples of manufactured, or synthetic fibers are nylon, polyester, microfiber, and Lycra. Some fabrics are a mix of both types.

Lycra and nylon are synthetic fibers.

Wool and silk are natural fibers.

The Business of Fashion

Designers work at least six months ahead of each season.

That means I'm designing swimwear in the middle of winter and big, woolly jackets when we're in the middle of a heat wave. I have to be very focused.

Big fashion houses can produce up to four collections per year, with an average of 70 garments per collection. Many more garments are made, but most are discarded. Only the very best will make it onto the catwalk.

Here at Hype, we have two collections per year—our winter and summer lines. For Fashion Week, I'm creating a fall line. I've decided that the theme for Hype's fall collection this year will be rock star style.

This dress made the final cut.

28

What does a fashion buyer do?

Fashion buyers work for large stores and buy collections of clothes to be sold in their stores. Buyers attend fashion shows all over the world to order clothes from both local and international designers.

Buyers must know the type of people who shop in their stores and predict the clothes they will want. They need a sharp eye to spot coming trends so they can buy clothes that will be in demand. Being a buyer, like being a sales manager, requires excellent communication skills and good business sense.

French for fashion

Haute couture is French for high fashion. This type of clothing consists of custom made pieces. A few exclusive fashion houses, like Chanel or Jean Paul Gaultier, create unique garments, made especially for individual (usually wealthy) clients. Expensive, high-quality materials and finishes are used.

Most designers create ready-to-wear (prêt-à-porter) clothing lines that are produced in various amounts and prices. Even couture houses make ready-to-wear lines to sell to the public.

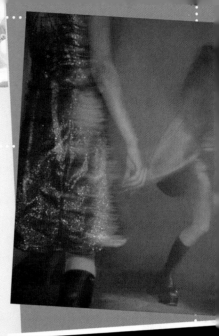

Organizing the Show

Why have a fashion show?

A fashion show gives me, as a designer, an opportunity to be creative and daring. I get to show how I would like my clothes to be worn.

A show is also a creative marketplace for buyers. They get to see the total idea of the clothes and how they can be worn. This helps them decide what they want to buy. Fashion magazine editors also get to see what designers are doing and what they have created for a future season.

Shows are very competitive. Buyers and magazine editors will only buy or review the best collections. A great show can mean being the talk of the town, with your clothes in all the top magazines. Soon after, everyone will want to wear them.

Fashion editors want the latest looks in their magazines.

Fashion is not just about clothes. It is also about style and image. A show is a fun way to present the style and image of the label as well as this season's theme. Shows are also an exciting way of building and marketing a fashion brand.

PUN FUN
Rich fashion designers have deep pockets.

ImOK

hype

sass & bide

Shows help make labels instantly recognizable.

I have hired Alex Johns to produce the Hype show. He is perfect for the job because he uses lots of color and drama. Alex's role is to make the show happen.

He puts together the lighting, music, and staging to create the show. It is important that everything reflect the mood of the clothes. I want the show to have the energy of a rock concert!

A good show producer will be bursting with ideas.

hype

Hype Fashion Show Countdown

June 18

I'm searching through piles of fabric samples, trying to choose which to use. It is very frustrating. We can't get enough of the fabric I really like, and another doesn't come in the color I need. I wonder whether there is time to dye it. I might not be able to get it delivered in time ... the search goes on.

I have the same problems with the trims. I spend lots of time asking questions like "Can I get that zipper in this color? Do you have these toggles in that style? What sizes are available for these buttons? How many of those beads can we get in time?"

Aargh! I can't find the perfect material!

>hype

Designing can be such a roller-coaster ride. One minute, I am feeling great, riding high on excitement about an idea. The next minute, I am confused and deflated as I run into problems trying to turn that idea into a reality.

June 27
Eventually I manage to find what I want, and I am riding high again. Most designers go through this. I guess it comes with wanting things to be just right.

I'm also doing research on the Internet trend sites for inspiration for the Hype look that I need to capture on my storyboards.

I imagine the collection will include ripped, tight jeans and vintage T-shirts. There'll be daring miniskirts, and accessories like looping metal wallet chains and lightning flash earrings.

A detailed color chart helps.

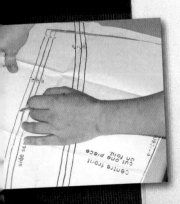

July 9
I am now well into the design process, and I'm madly sketching my ideas. It's sketching, sketching, and more sketching.

July 16
Things are starting to take shape. I'm drawing up some of the storyboards for the collection.

Storyboards are useful because they show how I want the clothes to look. They also have a sample of the fabrics and colors, so I can get an idea of the feel of the garments as well.

Aug. 6
Eva has begun to make patterns from my design sketches. Some fabric has already been cut so Julianna can start on the samples. This is when my ideas become reality—the exciting part!

Once Julianna has the sample garments ready, I will ask my part-time models, Noah and Skye, to come in and try them on.

Sept. 6
Skye and Noah model the samples. This is when we see how the garments fit the body for the first time. Are the legs too short or the sleeves too long? How about the waist? Is it too tight, too low, or too high?

We also get our first look at the finish of the clothes. Are the seams neat? Should they be double- or single-stitched? Does the fabric hang right? Do all the outside finishes on the garment, like pockets, buttonholes, and top stitching, match the style?

Well, this T-shirt looks good with a guitar on!

Sketches like this ...

... become style cards ...

... that end up as clothes like these!

Oct. 16

Now I'm finalizing the designs. Each design has a style number or name. I write up cards for each design that include a sketch and trim list, and have samples of fabric stapled to them. This way everyone can easily see by the cards what each design will look like.

Nov. 20

Everything is coming along well. We are all into a design routine: sample, make changes, new sample, send to seamstresses. I love this part.

Nov. 26

My life is a blur of fittings, fittings, fittings.

Dec. 3

Panic stations! Help!
I've lost my team! Eva and Ben are both sick. Robert is out producing news releases and organizing media coverage for the show. Meanwhile, Julianna is sewing at half pace, distracted because she is moving to a new house!

Fabrics have started to arrive, and stores are calling to reorder clothes from the last collection. There is SO much going on!

hype

Dec. 17
My pattern gurus are well again. Julianna has gotten her personal life under control, and everyone is back on track. Phew!

Zephyr: style guru

Robert finds a super stylist called Zephyr who will put together the look of the clothes for the catwalk. We have very similar ideas, and I'm thrilled when he books my favorite hairdresser, Stacey, and the makeup artist Madam β to do the models' hair and makeup. Perfect.

Madam B's a genius with makeup. What a score to get her!

I send the fabric to the cutters, where it will be cut, bundled, and sent on to the seamstresses to add all the trimmings. There are still so many things left to prepare.

Meeting in Progress!

Jan. 17
Half of January disappears
in meetings ... meetings ...
meetings ...

TYRONE

ALEX

VERONICA

I also spend hours with my team, sorting through the hundreds of model photos that have flooded in. We're picking the models for the show.

When the models are chosen, we ask them to come in. I decide who will wear what. The clothes are slightly altered so that all the clothes fit everyone perfectly. We take snapshots so we can remember what goes on whom!

ALISHA

Rehearsals for the show begin, and I send out the invitations.

Jan. 22
Only two weeks before the show. Everyone at Hype is working very long hours putting everything together and getting garments and accessories ready.

This is when I start to get nervous. The big day is looming. Will they like my concept? Will they like the clothes? Will everything be finished in time?

Jan. 29
Only seven days to go. Will we be ready? I keep worrying that I've forgotten something, but it looks as if we have everything under control. My collection is almost complete—just some last-minute, late-night adjustments to make.

Looks quiet now. Just wait 'til later!

Feb. 3—Two days to go!
I rush off to my last meeting with the Fashion Week organizers. Details like our guest list and the timing of the music and lights are discussed. To my relief, it's all agreed on without a hitch. Now what am I going to wear?

Feb. 5
THE DAY OF THE SHOW
The clothes are put into bundles for each of the models so everyone knows who is wearing what. They are pressed and hung on the racks along with all their accessories. That way the models can get changed as quickly as possible each time they come offstage.

Checking the stage

Time to put out the "reserved" signs.

Alex and I run through a quick last-minute rehearsal with the models, testing the music and lights. I am very nervous. The tension is high because some things are still not ready. We make changes right up to the last second. Everyone is tired but running on adrenaline with all the anticipation at the same time.

At the front, we are busy checking the chairs. There will be reserved seats for buyers, editors, and our special guests in the front rows. We want the buyers and editors up close, so they get the best view of the clothes.

Doing everyone's makeup takes hours.

As I rush backstage, Stacey and Madame B begin to work their magic with the models' hair and makeup. I'm sooo nervous! My stomach is full of butterflies.

This model is ready to go.

SHOW TIME!

7 P.M.—Lights! Music! Models! Action! The music starts. The house lights fade as the catwalk comes alive in a blaze of color. The models strut their stuff to the funky music. The butterflies in my stomach are replaced with excited energy as I watch from the side of the stage.

Backstage, it's a mad rush! Models changing, stylists working over-time, clothes flying everywhere. Onstage, everything looks cool and professional, going just as planned.

Good, everyone's got the right shoes!

I duck out the side to see the faces of the audience, but it's hard with all the lights swirling. I see the buyers and the fashion editors scribbling down notes. The photographers are snapping away. What are they thinking? Is it good or bad? I will know soon enough.

Everything is happening so fast. It's all a blur. Suddenly the show is over, and I walk onstage with all the models surrounding me. Everyone goes wild with applause. It's my moment in the spotlight, and I can't quite believe I'm here. Unreal!

Onstage it looks perfect.

There are lots of photographers here. Great!

Another one of my outfits being modeled for the cameras!

PUN FUN

He quit his job designing clothes to become a man of the cloth.

hYPE

Afterward I wander through the crowd and hear snippets of conversations:

"Fabulous!"

"This Hype collection is the best yet. It's fresh and exciting."

"Chloe's done it again!"

All the hard work has been worth it. Now it's time to celebrate!

I can't wait to order!

AFTER THE SHOW
Robert is ecstatic. His phone is ringing nonstop with buyers placing orders. We have five new overseas buyers interested in the collection. Fashion editors want comments, and fashion stylists are asking for pieces to use in photo shoots.

Wonderful! Brilliant!

I'm happy with the photo shoots.

Over the next few weeks, orders are confirmed with buyers and retailers. The collection goes into production so it can be in the stores by the beginning of the season for you to buy.

Now it's time for me to think of a new collection for the next season and start all over again!

I wonder what the next Hype collection will be like. Now let me think. . . .

43

Follow These Steps to Become a Fashion Designer

Step 1

Studying subjects like art, textiles, math, and business in high school will get you going in the direction to work in the fashion industry. This is also the time to start building up your skills in sketching, sewing, and pattern making.

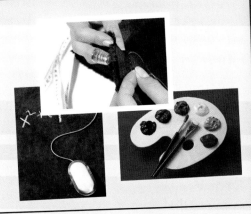

Step 2

Graduating from a vocational school or university with specialized training in fashion designing is recommended. Complementary courses in business administration, sales, and marketing will help you prepare for the job market.

Step 3

Building a design portfolio of your work is very important in getting a job as a fashion designer. People will want to see examples of your ideas and designs. Start collecting them now so you have something really special to show them! If you can, make your idea into a real piece of clothing.

Step 4

Once you get into the industry, you will be working from the bottom up. On the job, you'll learn many skills in the cutting room with the cutters and seamstresses. Expect hard work while you're learning, but also big rewards for all your efforts.

Step 5

Just as you need to have knowledge in so many varied areas, you will always need to be learning and updating your skills. You may also need to work long hours and be available around the clock, especially just before a big event.

Other opportunities in fashion

If you are interested in fashion, there are a variety of jobs that could be for you.

- **Fashion marketer or merchandiser**: Working on the business side of fashion, marketing the products or predicting trends
- **Jewelry maker**: Creating bracelets, earrings, necklaces, and other pieces
- **Tailor**: Sewing and altering clothes for individuals
- **Textile designer**: Creating designs for textiles
- **Theatrical costume designer and maker**: Producing costumes for stage or screen

Find Out More

In the Know

- Employment of fashion designers is projected to grow more slowly than the average for all occupations through 2014.

- Two-thirds of salaried fashion designers work in either New York or California.

- More than one in four fashion designers are self-employed.

- Employers want designers with a two- or four-year college degree who are knowledgeable about textiles, fabrics, trims, and fashion trends.

- The average annual pay for fashion designers in 2006 was $69,270. The lowest 10 percent earned less than $30,000, and the highest 10 percent earned more than $117,120.

Further Reading

Discovering Careers for Your Future: Fashion. New York: Ferguson, 2005.

Gaines, Ann. *Coco Chanel.* Philadelphia: Chelsea House, 2004.

Hantman, Clea. *I Wanna Make My Own Clothes.* New York: Aladdin Paperbacks, 2006.

Platt, Richard. *They Wore What?! The Weird History of Fashion and Beauty.* Minnetonka, Minn.: Two-Can, 2007.

Reeves, Diane Lindsey. *Career Ideas for Kids Who Like Art.* New York: Ferguson, 2007.

On the Web

For more information on this topic, use FactHound.

1. Go to *www.facthound.com*
2. Type in this book ID: 0756536227
3. Click on the *Fetch It* button.

Glossary

brand—a name that identifies a product or manufacturer, such as Adidas, Nike, or Levi

buyer—person who buys collections of clothes from designers to sell in his or her employer's stores

catwalk—a narrow walkway that models walk down during fashion shows

color scheme—colors chosen to be used together for clothes, interior design, or other purposes

concept—idea

garment—piece of clothing

grading—making garments in various sizes, such as small, medium, and large

invest—give money to a business in exchange for part ownership or part of the profits

production—the making of something

prototype—first trial model of something, made to test and improve the design

retailer—business that sells products to people for their own use

storyboard—collection of pictures and colors to show a designer's ideas

style book—book that shows the designs in the collection

textile—woven cloth or fabric

texture—the way something feels when you touch it

trademark—something that helps identify a company or person

trend forecast—prediction of what will be popular next season

Index

Look for More Books in This Series: